Chinese New Year, or Lunar New Year, marks the start of the lunar calendar. Families celebrate with feasts, honoring ancestors, and traditions to bring good luck. Each year is associated with one of 12 animals in the Chinese zodiac, adding special meaning to the celebration.

A NEW SUIT FOR A NEW YEAR

Sami, a six-year-old boy with bright eyes, gently smashed his piggy bank open, coins spilling everywhere. He'd saved every coin to buy a new outfit for the Lunar New Year. With his fluffy poodle wagging its tail beside him, Sami counted each coin, carefully stacking them with a proud smile.

Clutching his coins, Sami and his poodle eagerly headed to the bustling market, alive with red lanterns, vendors, and shoppers. At a shop window, a beautiful red suit caught Sami's eye-it was perfect! He counted his coins once more, feeling ready for this important purchase.

Proudly holding his new red suit in a plastic bag, Sami walked home, his puppy trotting alongside. The bright festival decorations around him made the street feel magical, and Sami couldn't wait to show his family his special outfit for the New Year celebration.

SNAKES EVERYWHERE!

On the way home, Sami noticed something surprising-snake decorations everywhere! From walls to cakes, snakes seemed to be the main theme. Sami scratched his head, wondering why it wasn't dragons this year.

Passing a group of laughing kids holding paper snakes, Sami overheard them talking about the "Year of the Snake." His curiosity grew even more-what did it all mean? He hurried home, hoping someone could explain.

At home, Sami asked his sister about the snakes. Smiling, she explained that every year in the Chinese zodiac is represented by a different animal. Last year was the dragon, and this year was the snake! Sami's face lit up with excitement as he finally understood.

LEARNING THE SNAKE DANCE

Inspired, Sami decided he would learn a snake dance to celebrate! He imagined moving smoothly like a snake, impressing everyone at the festival. He practiced in his room, his poodle watching curiously.

Sami stretched his arms, twisting his body like a snake while his poodle barked playfully. His sister cheered him on, laughing as Sami tried his best to look like a real snake.

After practicing, Sami looked at his reflection in his new red suit, feeling ready to perform. He smiled confidently, proud of his hard work, and couldn't wait to share his dance with everyone.

A FESTIVAL TO REMEMBER

Finally, the festival night arrived! Dressed in his new suit, Sami joined the crowd of people celebrating under red lanterns. The air was alive with music and laughter, and Sami felt thrilled.

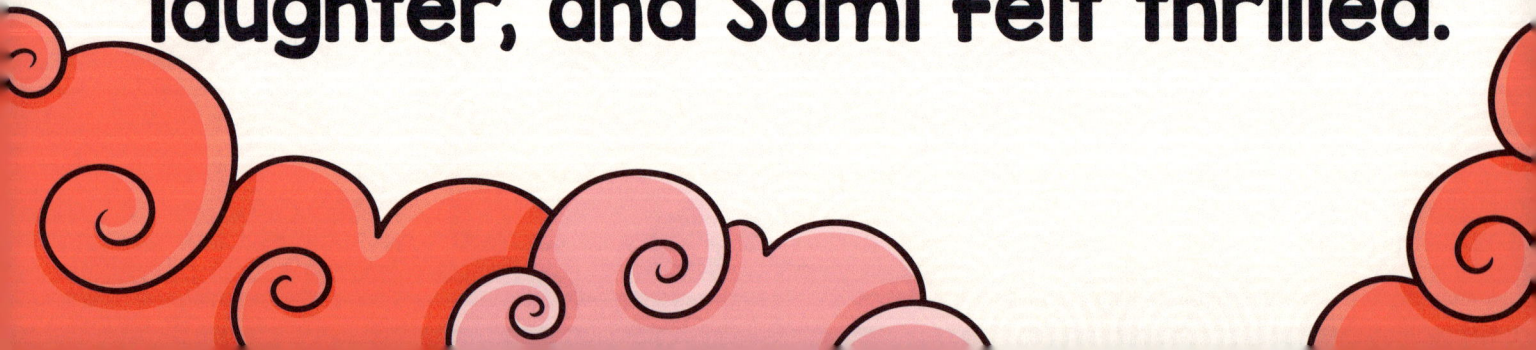

When the drums began, Sami danced, moving like a snake with grace. The crowd clapped and cheered, impressed by his performance. His sister cheered in the front row, proud of her brother's special dance.

As the crowd cheered, Sami beamed with pride. His heart felt full as he shouted, "Happy Year of the Snake!" Knowing he'd made this festival unforgettable, he felt the joy of the New Year.

Circle the Correct Answer!